SHADOWS
TO
DAYLIGHT

SHADOWS TO DAYLIGHT

REVEREND CARL YOUNT

Shadows to Daylight

Copyright © 2021 by Reverend Carl Yount. All rights reserved.

No part of this publication may be reproduced, stored in a retrieval system or transmitted in any way by any means, electronic, mechanical, photocopy, recording or otherwise without the prior permission of the author except as provided by USA copyright law.

The opinions expressed by the author are not necessarily those of URLink Print and Media.

1603 Capitol Ave., Suite 310 Cheyenne, Wyoming USA 82001
1-888-980-6523 | admin@urlinkpublishing.com

URLink Print and Media is committed to excellence in the publishing industry.

Book design copyright © 2021 by URLink Print and Media. All rights reserved.

Published in the United States of America

Library of Congress Control Number: 2021920282
ISBN 978-1-64753-985-6 (Paperback)
ISBN 978-1-64753-986-3 (Hardback)
ISBN 978-1-64753-987-0 (Digital)

16.08.21

CONTENTS

Morning Reflection 7
Ironhorse Bike Blessing 2012 9
Faith in The Big Bang 11
Marriage Blessing 13
I See You Got My Message 15
A Creed Of Conviction 19
Blessing For Coming Of Age 21
The Importance of the Superego 22
Ironhorses Blessing 2013 25
Who Am I? 27
Blessing Of Gathering 29
The Thisle 31
Burial Prayer 33
Do Not Weep, Rejoice 35
Should God be held Accountable? 36
Blessing Of A Meal 39
The Prophet's Light 40
Prayers for service persons 43
Prayer for the sick and ill 45
Adversity 46
A Prayer Of Adversity 49
Bike Blessing 51
Evening Reflections 53

MORNING REFLECTION

Oh Lord on high
With thanks to thee
I wake this day
And with the dawning of anew light
With faith in thee I rise and pray

I know you meet me
with the rise of the sun
And guide me through
The day we have won

I ask you for thy wisdom and strength
To guide me as I lead
And plant thy knowledge of faith
In the heart of others as a seed

Please help me make correct choices
As I try not to wrong others on my path
And help lead me peacefully past
The mislead chose of others wrath

Oh Lord please help to calm the rivers flow
When I need to set down to rest
And lay me down in the bounty
Of thy limbs and crest

IRONHORSE BIKE BLESSING
2012

In the name of our Lord
As a family united in one
We come now together
In the blessing of the sun

As brothers and sisters
Of a kindred soul
Down the highway
We shall roll

Let the road rise before us
Free of trouble and harm
As we ride together
In life's beauty and charm

May the Lord be watchful
And guide us on our way
As we are blessed by the glory
Of another bountiful day

So let us ride forth
As we ask the Lord to bless our steed
As we may enjoy this day
And were it may lead

FAITH IN THE BIG BANG

Asked by a man about "God "and creation, he said if I have faith in the existence of a divinity that as responsible for creation then I must not give to the "Big Bang Theory". Not wanting to get into the definition of the word "theory" I simply replied "I don't know how God did it, I wasn't there".

Part of the joke to this is that the big bang theory is extremely accepted and used throughout science, science fiction and fiction. TV shows and movies refer to the big bang theory repeatedly as if it were "the big bang fact". Well the word "fact" is not in there.

"Faith" the believe in something regardless of the "facts" that support or dispute the believe in it. Faith in a divinity responsible for the creation of all we know to be the universe is supposed to be in dispute with the big bang theory, but the truth is there is not enough evidence to prove or disprove this very theory so many have chosen to have "faith" in its assumption. Aristotle theorized that every action results in a reaction. If you follow every reaction back to the causing action you would eventually arrive at the original action, or other wise you would find the face of God. No theory exploits this idea more then the "big bang theory".

So in conclusion the only fact to conclude in this new found faith in a scientific assumption is that man needs faith in God's existents even in the attempt to prove God dose not exist.

MARRIAGE BLESSING

Oh Lord with the wisdom
of your light
help us see through
the darkness of our sight

Oh Lord bless this union
in all your wisdom and grace
lead them down there path
together in loves embrace

Help guide these two
in the joy of wedded flight
as they keep each other from straying
into the darkness of eternal night

Keep them together in your arms
and tight in your wishes range
as with rings and vows
in there heart they exchange

And Lord we ask in your divine light
and with whole hearted love
that you watch over there union in kind
and embrace them as your dove

I SEE YOU GOT MY MESSAGE

The Simple Man

In the still of the countryside sits a cottage plank and plain. A man of simple life is seen there tilling a small garden, then feeds his chickens, sheep, and goat. Then quietly milks his cow and tends to her calf. All awhile his dog fouls as his aid and companion.

He knows not of books to read or the business of his distant neighbors.

Through if one wonders by he's sure to great them with a pleasant smile and a wave.

"If You Feed the Hungry"

One night as he stands looking out the window at his small garden and the creatures he tends to each day. Then with a smile he stands prod to say "though I don't have much I am blessed, for I don't know what it is to wont." Then he turns to sit down to his dinner.

A knock comes to the door. When he opens it, he sees a woman standing there. As she looks to him she pleads, "please kind sir, I have traveled far and have no food." Looking upon her gentle he replies "My dinner is hot and waiting, please eat and feast. I will eat tomorrow."

"If You Cloth the Naked"

A couple of nights later as the man looks out the window and again said "though I don't have much I am blessed, for I don't know what it is to want." Then again he hears a knock at the door. When he opens the door he sees a man standing there, bruised and naked. "Please kind sir, I was beaten and robbed by thugs. They took every thing, even my clothes."

The man promptly gave him his shirt and pants he was wearing, and then wrapped himself in a blanket. Then handed the man his shoes saying "these maybe old and worn but they will carry you to town."

"If You Shelter the Homeless"

A couple of nights later as the man looks out the window and again sees "though I don't have much I am blessed, for I don't know what it is to want." Then again he hears a knock at the door, and this time he finds a young couple standing there. "Please kind sir, I and my wife where abruptly through out of our apartment. Could you give us logging for the night?" The man replies in kindness "you may take my bed to use as you need. I will lay on the floor with my dog, she will keep me warm."

"You Got My Message"

Time passes and the man is old. A night comes that Death comes to greet the man in his sleep. Death then takes him to stand before the gates of heaven, where he sees a man waiting for him. The stranger to him walks up and embraces him tightly and said "Welcome Brother, I see you got my message."

A CREED OF CONVICTION

The Lord is my shadow
I shall not need.
She teaches me to follow
so I may lead.

She takes me through
the valley of death.
So I may know
the evil in my breath

She leads me to rapid waters
and calms their flow
So I may lead others
Into the light of faith's glow

She is my guide
and light of day
I am her servant
as a child of clay.

She teaches me to forgive
The trespasses I endure
As I pay the penance for the
trespasses I commit and more.

Armed with sword and word
I shall ride out and teach
As with her guidance
Into their hearts we shall reach.

BLESSING FOR COMING OF AGE

In the name of our Lord
As a family united in one
We come now together
In the blessing of the sun

To celebrate the special thing
Of those who now come of age
And help to guide there path
As now they prepare to engage

We now give thanks to those
that have laid their faith down
As we take of there bounty
And together bare there crown

As a family united
In the spirit of endless sight
We give thanks to the Lord
In all heavenly might

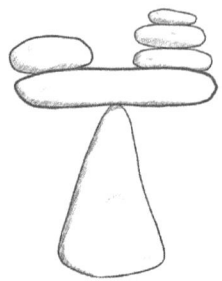

THE IMPORTANCE OF THE SUPEREGO

In other sermons I talk of "God, Allah, and Gaia etc..." As a concept, a name we use to conceive the inconceivable. But regardless faith is the belief in that which we can not conceive and the acceptance that it is and always was and shall be.

Though today faith falters as people lose value in that which they try to conceive, faith becomes an empty echo of what their parents did and their parents before them did. All this I talk about in other sermons so lets move on.

If we look at nature as the Id, the part which acts most basic, the primitive part of the whole, food, shelter, and reproduce. Man as the ego, the moral fibers and freewill which separate man from 'beast'. Since the day we took part in tasting the fruit of the tree of knowledge of good and evil we have risen above our natural drives and needs and accept the reasonability that comes with such a status. This is not my point, this about the importance of faith and "God" as the superego.

The superego is the balance between the Id and the ego, as we expand our knowledge of the universe we loose the mystery that is the need for God. But as well with the loss of God, we loose our connection with nature, the more technology expands and our "attack on nature" continues the more nature strikes back. Without God to balance the conflict the more destructive the cycle continues to become.

With faith in God and understanding of creation and no matter what Science tells us there is intelligence beyond our comprehension that is responsible for the universe and all its "wonders". Friedrich Nietzsche stated that with the loss of moral turpitude we are killing God; I'm not so sure he was wrong.

IRONHORSES BLESSING 2013

Oh Lord with the wisdom
Of your light
Help us see through
The darkness of our sight

As we venture forth
On this glorious day
For your guidance we seek
For your wisdom we pray

As our kickstands are lifted
And our journey begins anew
Our brotherly and sisterly love
In your love is true

May the road rise before us
And our troubles fall behind
May you guide us to the treasures
We wish to find

So we let your glow lead us
In health and prayer

WHO AM I?

Who am I that at
Heaven's Gate shall stand
stalled and still like a dream
held my in hand

I dream of life
lead and cast
into the future
the very moments of the past

A past of slipping through
a shadow of life
were born by fate
and madness my wife

A fate predetermined
by desire and fear
where I walk the coast
by a cold pond so sincere

A pond so cold
it burns my path
that flooded with wine
into the glass of my epitaph

A wine so rich
and thick with blood
it stained my dream
as it pulled me down into the flood

A dream that made
me feel alive and burst
but started by an
unquenchable thirst

A thirst for time
and endless space
but walled in a maze
red round by my pace

Streams that lead
to the shore
and in my heart
life with faith shall pour

BLESSING OF GATHERING

Oh Lord with the wisdom
of your light
Help us see through
the darkness of our sight

Help us let your wisdom
guide us in decisions made
As we gather together our worry
in your presence shall fade

Please lead our thoughts down
there truest trail
As into our venture
we shall sail

Oh Lord within you we place
our faith and love
Lead us forth with the blessing of
thy heaven sent dove

And let us go forth from this gathering
of sisters and brothers in your name
As we shall speak put in your love
and in our faith show no shame

As into the path of your glory
Our faith shall tare

THE THISLE

The sun bleeds down
upon the swaying shafts of wheat
a breeze conversing their dance
as they sat witnessing in their seat

An abrupt shutter brings a split
in both earth and air
as a thistle rises up
with a stagnant flare

It sways not with
the coursing breeze
but rather of the moment
it tries to seize

Poke irritably at the closest shafts
with a boisterous boast
stealing time from the
moment's host

But when the harvest comes
the wheat is gathered
the thistle shall be left
weathered and tattered

Laid silent and alone
and avoid of decision
the thistle overshadowed
by its own envision

BURIAL PRAYER

Oh Heavenly Father, we gather to lay to rest our friend, companion, and family member, as we know thy love is so great that no sparrow shall fall but what is known in heaven. We know that it is with understanding you look upon this scene today. When that which is so loved as this pet is loved by its family, is gone unto your grace.

Ever loyal, ever faithful, and ever loving, may we as we leave this service promise to our Lord and others that we too will be more loyal, more faithful, and more loving. As we need to do those things which will hasten the coming of they kingdom.

Please give us strength, for we ask it in thy name that you watch over his/her spirit

Until we meet again.

DO NOT WEEP, REJOICE

A PRAYER OF ASCENSION

Do not weep for I am not gone
Rejoice for I have ascended
into dream

Rejoice for I risen into the kingdom
Of our Lord (God)

Rejoice for I now sit up at his table

Rejoice for all that is my misery
I have taken with me

Rejoice for all that is my pain
I have shed

Do not weep as in it's time we shall be united
At the gates of love and harmony
Do not weep for we have never parted

And together
We shall shed our sorrow

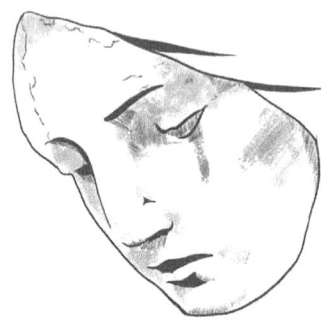

SHOULD GOD BE HELD ACCOUNTABLE?

Recently in a discussion about the bible we came to a disagreement of opinion. When ask if I did not see the Bible as the "word of God" I had to respond with the apparent evidence that it has been altered by too many people (politicians an like) over the century's. To which was replied "would God let that happen?"

Would God let that happen? Would God let the serpent tempt Eve? Would God let an act of infidelity result in the enslavement of an entire race? Would God let a "good catholic boy "try to exterminate another entire race because the Bible holds them responsible for the death of Jesus?

Would God let this happen!? Hell of a question. If God had that sort of control "freewill" would be a myth and God could be held accountable for ALL the wrongs and suffering that we witness every day.

In another conversation between two members of a Bible study group as they where discussing dismissing members that didn't use the "right" Bible!

Now we have "the right Bible" would God let this happen?! If God keeps the bible from being altered, how do we have so many versions? Wouldn't there only be one? And which one would that be?

A friend of mine shared his latest obsession by sharing several videos of atomic explosions. He found the power of the event exhilarating. I myself found it disturbing, to see the destruction and death, frankly the row power of a god. Or more accurately I saw the death of God in the blink of an eye. If God could keep us from changing one book why would it let us split the very building blocks of the universe to release this power only a God should have? So then we can hold God accountable for the death of 200,000 men women and children in Japan during World War 2.

Questions raised are simple the answers are found in all versions of the Bible, the Torah and even the Koran (plus many other rescore books). We have free will, and with freewill come reasonability. And finally we are not to try making God accountable for the wrongs we do to one another.

When researching any one subject it is best to use ALL source material available and remember that the authors (including myself) tend to subjectively the materials with there own ideas. I myself have found to cross reference two or more different bibles and other books helpful.

BLESSING OF A MEAL

Oh Lord bless this gathering
Of friends and family bound
As in your vision we come together
And in your light are found

Please bless this bounty
We are about to share
As in your wisdom we know
Each other's love and care

And bring to us
Your knowledge and light
That we may share together the truth
And meaning of this very night

To hold tight the family
And cherish our bond of love
As in our hearts you have
laid the seeds of the golden dove

And let us give thanks to
the spirits now are in your grace
that gave up their time here so we may take
of this bounty in this place

THE PROPHET'S LIGHT

"Neither a pawn nor a king, but a rook that comes in the night"

A good leader must know both how to lead as well as follow. One who is open to the calling as a prophet must know the importance of choosing their council (disciples) and help them see the wrong in our actions and correct ours while respecting the rights of others. It is also important to teach respect for the rituals of there faith while they celebrate in new ideas.

"If a blind man leads the blind they both will fall into the hole"

A true prophet of "God" must learn how to ascend the plains of ignorant and the mortal desires' to see clearly into the aeons of ancestral enlightenment. To do this one must open their hearts soul to the light of the spirit and embrace that which is "God's" breathe within us. Only then can the prophet begin to understand both the truth and the lies, but more important the true that is in the lies. To teach the knowledge of the ages one must know of the books and writings both earthly and in the aeons as you learn to read them with an open spirit.

> "You must embrace the darkness, for if
> you embrace it, you control it,
> if you fear it, it controls you"

The prophet must recognize that there is never darkness in a person's heart but rather it may surround them, and by embracing them you reach though the darkness to open your heart's soul to "God's" embrace. For we do not do "God's" work, "God works through us!

> "The one eyed man in the land of the blind
> Shall be deemed the village idiot"

The prophet must understand the truth that if you speak out against the common opinion or try to introduce ideas people don't want to understand the results can be unappealing. Just ask Gondi, Marten Luther king Jr., and of course Jesus of Nazareth.

The true Prophet is not the one to give us the answer but rather the ONE to help us find the question, The True Prophet is the ONE that stops us from looking to the heavens but rather guides us in to our own heart's soul to seek the truth

> "GOD'S" loves is how we love ourselves
> "GOD'S" mercy is how we treat each other
> "God" is not only Father Son and Holy Ghost
> But rather the true trinity
> (Man, Nature, and Divinity)

PRAYERS FOR SERVICE PERSONS

R) Oh Lord we humbly ask your thanks for those who of themselves give

So we may in tranquility live

That you may watch over them and keep them safe in both your glory and love as they watch over us and our families as you watchful dove

C) O Lord hear our prayers

PRAYER FOR THE SICK AND ILL

R) O Lord as we gather in this right

   As we stand in the glory your light

   Please guide us wisely with your sight

C) Hear our prayers

R) We ask thy blessing and mercy for those

   Who have fallen sick and taken ill

   As you may see them well and guide them with your wisdom and will

C) Hear our prayers

R) O Lord we ask of you in mortal plea

   As we trust in you in all your glee

   And hold witness to your glory

C) O Lord share thy mercy.

   (names called out by congregation)

ADVERSITY

We ask why God chooses to strike down such good people forgetting that God has nothing to do with it. They say God created the world and plans everything that happens here, a statement of half truth.

God created the world and has a plan we are not developed enough to understand. God did not take six days to paint a still life portrait and then take the rest of eternity off. God spent six days laying the foundation for an epic poem rested on the seventh and then has been hard at work with the creation of this epic poem ever since the eighth day started.

Why do these things happen? The two greatest gifts God gave us are life, God's breath and unconditional love, the other is free will and the choice to return that love to God unconditionally. The foundation is nature (those things God willed into being but has limited control) you can build a fountain but you can't control the route and fate that every drop of water takes, and man to which was given free will so we can choose to receive Gods love freely and can choose to respond with our love freely.

The epic poem is life, and what is life if not uncontrollable exhilarating, and yes some times tragic. God doesn't make these things happen but we need love and trust enough to believe God is with us before during and after, warning, guiding and helping.

We shall never forget "the footprints in the sand."

A PRAYER OF ADVERSITY

Creator of all
In this our hour of need
We turn to you as loves fertile seed
And trust in your wisdom
The path on which you lead

Oh divine host
We know they will be great
They love shall clean the slate
As with your guides in our hearts
We shall despond our hate

We trust in thee
To dry the wrath of rain
To clear our hearts of pain
To wash away the anger and rage
That in our soul does stain

We ask of thee
To give us strength for another day
And help us stand proud to pray
And in your love from your path
Do not let us stray

Oh that which is on high
Your love shall dry our tear's end
Your compassion shall help us ascend
As with your wisdom and guidance
shall help us find the strength to mend

BIKE BLESSING

All on high
We ask as you look upon
This humble group of souls
On this glorious day you help us each
With our various goals

That you give us your blessing
Strength and light
Keep us held in your
Embrace so tight

Watch over our family and friends
And keep them from pain
And keep safe those who Fight over seas
So our freedom dose rain

Help our decisions be wise
and aid us in our flight
as we ride on knowing
your grace and might

Oh Lord;
Of your wisdom, strength,
and glory's reach
To you in humble plea
your love and mercy we beseech

EVENING REFLECTIONS

Of all that is Divine
I thank thee
for the day now done
As with thee
we behold the setting sun

I thank thee for the strength
to change that which we need to change
I thank thee for the tolerance
to except that which we cannot change
And I ask thee for the wisdom
to know the different

As now you lay my mind down
to ease and rest
Upon the warmth of
your loving breast
As tomorrow I may rise
to bare your wisdom and crest

www.ingramcontent.com/pod-product-compliance
Ingram Content Group UK Ltd.
Pitfield, Milton Keynes, MK11 3LW, UK
UKHW022218230426
12048UKWH00016BA/931